Union in Christ

A Declaration for the Church

Union in Christ
A Declaration for the Church

A Commentary with Questions for Study and Reflection

Andrew Purves
Mark Achtemeier

Unless otherwise noted, Scripture quotations are from the New Revised Standard Version of the Bible, copyright © 1989 by the Division of Christian Education of the National Council of the Churches of Christ in the U.S.A. Used by permission.

Every effort has been made to trace copyrights on the materials included in this book. If any copyrighted material has nevertheless been included without permission and due acknowledgment, proper credit will be inserted in future printings after notice has been received.

Edited by Frank T. Hainer

Book interior and cover design by Pip Pullen

Cover Art: Coptic Icon of Christ Contemporary, Ecumenical Center, Geneva, Switzerland

First edition

Published by Witherspoon Press, a Ministry of the General Assembly Council, Congregational Ministries Division, Presbyterian Church (U.S.A.), Louisville, Kentucky

Web site address: http://www.pcusa.org/pcusa/witherspoon

PRINTED IN THE UNITED STATES OF AMERICA

99 00 01 02 03 04 05 06 07 08 — 10 9 8 7 6 5 4 3 2 1

Library of Congress Cataloging-in-Publication Data

Achtemeier, Mark, date.
   Union in Christ : a declaration for the church / Mark Achtemeier and Andrew Purves. — 1st ed.
      p.   cm.
   Includes bibliographical references.
   ISBN 1-57153-019-3
    1. Presbyterian Church (U.S.A.) Union in Christ. 2. Presbyterian Church (U.S.A.) — Doctrines. 3. Presbyterian Church (U.S.A.) — Discipline.
   I. Purves, Andrew, date- . II. Title.
   BX8969.5.P743A34 1999
   230'. 5137—dc21
                                        99-25892

Dedicated to Thomas F. Torrance,
theologian and churchman,
with gratitude.

Contents

Foreword ix

Preface xi

Union in Christ: A Declaration for the Church xiii

Introduction 1

Section I. Confessing Jesus Christ 9

Section II. The Work of the Trinity in the Life
of the Church 19

Section III. Our Life in Christ 33

Section IV. Christ's Life in Us 47

Section V. The Church as the Body of Christ 57

About the Authors 70

Foreword

Union in Christ: A Declaration for the Church is not a statement of faith of the Presbyterian Church (U.S.A.). It is not part of the Church's *Book of Confessions* and it has no authoritative place in the Church's faith and life. It is not an expression of the Church's representative presbyteries, synods, or the General Assembly. Why, then, is Witherspoon Press publishing the text of *Union in Christ* together with a commentary and questions?

Though not an official Church statement, *Union in Christ* is, nevertheless, a considered statement of faith and worthy of study and reflection by thoughtful Christians. Indeed, as such it stands in a long line of faith statements in the Reformed tradition. Reformed Christians have always been confession-making people, giving formal testimony to their faith in a variety of times, places, and contexts. In the sixteenth century alone more than sixty confessions were produced by Reformed churches. The World Alliance of Reformed Churches has published a representative collection of more than twenty-five Reformed confessions from the twentieth century.

The great variety of Reformed confessions is not a mere accident of history and geography. Reformed Christians have always believed that the Church is called to give testimony to its faith and action in every time and place. This call to confess faith is coupled with an emphasis on the sovereignty of God, leading to an acute awareness of the danger of idolatry, including the idolatry of creeds. That is why Reformed churches rarely identify a single historic confession as *the* authoritative expression of Christian faith.

In the Reformed tradition, formulation of confessions is understood as one response to the Church's mandate of proclamation. The need for *present* witness to the gospel has always been a feature of ecclesiastical existence. "In every age, the church has expressed its witness in words and deeds as the need of the time required. . . . No one type of confession is exclusively valid, no one statement is irreformable" (*Confession of 1967*, 9.02-03).

While not a statement of the whole Church, *Union in Christ* is a declaration of faith that has grown out of a significant gathering of Presbyterians. It is an important contribution to the Church's ongoing conversation about its faith and life. The commentary and study questions will be useful to the whole Church as it seeks to grow in faith, hope, and love.

Joseph Small
Director
Office of Theology and Worship
Presbyterian Church (U.S.A.)

Preface

The following is a series of notes and reflections on the text of *Union in Christ: A Declaration for the Church.* Our purpose in offering these reflections is twofold. First, we want to assist in the process of understanding the Declaration. Our hope is that our readers will develop a better understanding of both the theology that underlies the text of the Declaration and the analysis of the contemporary situation that informed its composition.

Second, our hope is that the discussions presented here will give readers a starting point for their own reflection on the implications for a Church life that arise out of the text of *Union in Christ.* We want to emphasize that this presentation is not an "authoritative interpretation" of the text; nor is it an exhaustive statement of the practical implications of the affirmations and denials contained in the Declaration.

The positions taken here are our own and do not necessarily represent views either held or officially endorsed by other members of the

Presbyterian Coalition. Some of the implications we have drawn from the text may well strike some readers as controversial, if not positively misguided, and we welcome serious response to them. Our intention is to open up discussion around the text of the Declaration, not to close it down. If this document succeeds, in concert with the Declaration, in provoking serious theological discussion within the Presbyterian Church over the content and implications of our biblical and Reformed Christian faith, our hopes for this project will have been more than amply fulfilled.

We have benefitted greatly from the insights and suggestions of many friends and colleagues on the Visioning and Refinement Teams of the Presbyterian Coalition, as well as from numerous individuals across the country who have submitted feedback concerning the text of the Declaration. For what is helpful in this work we owe a great debt to these collaborators. For what is mistaken or unhelpful the full responsibility is ours.

Mark Achtemeier
Andrew Purves

Union in Christ:
A Declaration
for the Church

He himself is before all things, and in him all things hold together.
(Col. 1:17)

With the witness of Scripture and the Church through the ages we declare:

I

Jesus Christ is the gracious mission of God
 to the world
 and for the world.
He is Emmanuel and Savior,
One with the Father,
God incarnate as Mary's son,
Lord of all,
The truly human one.

His coming transforms everything.
His Lordship casts down every idolatrous claim to authority.
His incarnation discloses the only path to God.
His life shows what it means to be human.
His atoning death reveals the depth of God's love for sinners.
His bodily resurrection shatters the powers of sin and death.

II

The Holy Spirit joins us to Jesus Christ by grace alone, uniting our life with his through the ministry of the Church.

> In the proclamation of the Word, the Spirit calls us to repentance, builds up and renews our life in Christ, strengthens our faith, empowers our service, gladdens our hearts, and transforms our lives more fully into the image of Christ.

>> We turn away from forms of Church life that ignore the need for repentance, that discount the transforming power of the Gospel, or that fail to pray, hope, and strive for a life that is pleasing to God.

> In Baptism and conversion the Spirit engrafts us into Christ, establishing the Church's unity and binding us to one another in him.

>> We turn away from forms of Church life that seek unity in theological pluralism, relativism, or syncretism.

> In the Lord's Supper the Spirit nurtures and nourishes our participation in Christ and our communion with one another in him.

>> We turn away from forms of Church life that allow human divisions of race, gender, nationality, or economic class to mar the Eucharistic fellowship, as though in Christ there were still walls of separation dividing the human family.

III

Engrafted into Jesus Christ we participate through faith in his relationship with the Father.

> By our union with Christ we participate in his righteousness before God, even as he becomes the bearer of our sin.
>
> > We turn away from any claim to stand before God apart from Christ's own righteous obedience, manifest in his life and sacrifice for our sake on the cross.
>
> By our union with Christ we participate in his knowledge of the Father, given to us as the gift of faith through the unique and authoritative witness of the Old and New Testaments.
>
> > We turn away from forms of Church life that discount the authority of Scripture or claim knowledge of God that is contrary to the full testimony of Scripture as interpreted by the Holy Spirit working in and through the community of faith across time.
>
> By our union with Christ we participate in his love of the Father, manifest in his obedience "even unto death on the cross."
>
> > We turn away from any supposed love of God that is manifest apart from a continual longing for and striving after that loving obedience which Christ offers to God on our behalf.

IV

Though obscured by our sin, our union with Christ causes his life to shine forth in our lives. This transformation of our lives into the image of Christ is a work of the Holy Spirit begun in this life as a sign and promise of its completion in the life to come.

> By our union with Christ our lives participate in the holiness of the One who fulfilled the Law of God on our behalf.

We turn away from forms of Church life that ignore Christ's call to a life of holiness, or that seek to pit Law and Gospel against one another as if both were not expressions of the one Word of God.

By our union with Christ we participate in his obedience. In these times of moral and sexual confusion we affirm the consistent teaching of Scripture that calls us to chastity outside of marriage and faithfulness within the covenant of marriage between a man and a woman.

We turn away from forms of Church life that fail to pray for and strive after a rightly ordered sexuality as the gracious gift of a loving God, offered to us in Christ by the power of the Holy Spirit. We also turn away from forms of Church life that fail to forgive and restore those who repent of sexual and other sins.

V

As the body of Christ the Church has her life in Christ.

By our union with Christ the Church binds together believers in every time and place.

We turn away from forms of Church life that identify the true Church only with particular styles of worship, polity, or institutional structure. We also turn away from forms of Church life that ignore the witness of those who have gone before us.

By our union with Christ the Church is called out into particular communities of worship and mission.

We turn away from forms of Church life that see the work of the local congregation as sufficient unto itself, as if it were not a local representation of the one, holy, catholic, and apostolic Church called together by the power of the Spirit in every age and time until our Lord returns.

By our union with Christ our lives participate in God's mission to the world:

> to uphold the value of every human life,
> to make disciples of all peoples,
> to establish Christ's justice and peace in all creation,
> and to secure that visible oneness in Christ that is the
>   promised inheritance of every believer.

> We turn away from forms of Church life that fail to bear witness in word and deed to Christ's compassion and peace, and the Gospel of salvation.

By our union with Christ the Church participates in Christ's resurrected life and awaits in hope the future that God has prepared for her. Even so come quickly, Lord Jesus!

In the name of the Father, and of the Son, and of the Holy Spirit.

Introduction

How the Declaration Came to Be

The Gathering of Presbyterians II, which met in Dallas, Texas, in the fall of 1997, issued a resounding call for renewal within the Presbyterian Church (U.S.A.). The immediate context was a Church whose unity was gravely threatened, whose common life was disrupted by conflict and mistrust, and whose mission was hampered by a sense of alienation between the people in the pews and the denomination's leadership. The participants at the Dallas gathering concluded that *confession* of the Church's faith was an essential ingredient in any effort to renew the life of the denomination.

Recognizing and affirming the tremendous resource available to the Church in the *Book of Confessions*, participants at the second Dallas gathering felt the need for a fresh declaration of faith that would speak in a compelling way to contemporary challenges facing the Church. Such a statement could serve as a rallying point for uniting the various renewal movements and help Presbyterians to reclaim the treasures of their confessional and doctrinal heritage. In the winter of 1997–1998 a sixteen-person Visioning Team was appointed and commissioned to write a declaration of faith and a strategy for renewal. *Union in Christ: A Declaration for the Church* is the faith statement that resulted from that initiative.

After an extensive review process, the text of the Declaration was finalized at the Gathering of Presbyterians III, meeting in Dallas, Texas, in October 1998. The six hundred delegates attending that conference pledged themselves to promote the theology set forth in the Declaration and to teach and proclaim it in their churches. This commentary with questions for study and reflection is one part of the effort growing out of Gathering III to make the Declaration available as a teaching document in local congregations.

Declaration versus Confession

The Declaration seeks to explore implications of a *single* theological theme—the believer's union with Christ—for the contemporary Church. This means that while the Declaration makes significant claims about the content of Christian faith, it is not intended to be a comprehensive statement that touches on every aspect of Christian belief.

There is an important distinction between a *confession* and a *declaration* of faith. A *confession* seeks to present a comprehensive summary of all the essential doctrines of Christian faith, whereas a *declaration* seeks only to lift up certain elements of the faith in order to speak to a particular situation. Examples of confessional statements in our *Book of Confessions* (hereafter *BOC*) include *The Heidelberg Catechism*, *The Second Helvetic Confession*, and *The Westminster Confession*, all of which seek to summarize in comprehensive fashion the essential elements of Christian faith. The clearest example of a declaration in the present *BOC* is the *Theological Declaration of Barmen*, which used a few very particular elements of Christian faith to address the situation faced by the German Confessing Church in Nazi Germany.

Intermediate forms between declarations and confessions are possible. One might argue, for example, that *The Confession of 1967* would be more aptly named the *"Declaration of 1967,"* since its major focus is the application of one particular aspect of Christian faith (the ministry of reconciliation) to the issues of racial and social justice confronting the American Church in the 1960s.

These ambiguous cases notwithstanding, it is important to keep clear the distinction between a declaration and a confession in the current instance. In a theological declaration, the fact that some area of doctrine gets left out of the document does *not* mean that we think it nonessential or unimportant; it only means that such matters do not fall within the limited scope of the document's concern. So, for example, the fact that there is only brief and passing reference to the sacraments in the *Theological Declaration of Barmen* does *not* mean that the framers of that document thought the sacraments unimportant or incidental to the life of the Church. It only means that a detailed discussion of the sacraments was not an essential element in the statement they felt the faithful churches had to make in the context of Hitler's Germany. Similarly in the present instance, the fact that the Declaration contains no explicit reference to the doctrine of providence, for example, does *not* mean we think that doctrine unimportant to Christian faith. A declaration, by its nature, should be interpreted on the basis of the positive statements it makes rather than what it leaves out.

What the Declaration Tries to Do

The Declaration does not seek to develop a "new" theology or to depart significantly from the broad currents of Reformed faith represented in the *Book of Confessions*. Rather, it tries to restate in a fresh way aspects of the Church's historic faith that speak to challenges facing the Presbyterian Church (U.S.A.) in these days. Five challenges in particular stand at the center: the challenge of *Christology* (this is the theological term that addresses "what we think about Jesus"), the challenge of *discipleship*, the challenge of *authority*, the challenge of *mission*, and the challenge of *Church unity*.

Regarding *Christology*, it is clear that a key element in the crisis facing the Presbyterian Church (U.S.A.) is the question that Jesus himself put to his disciples: "Who do you say that I am?" Doubts and misgivings about Jesus' singular saving Lordship and divinity have appeared at every level of the Church's life. The Declaration responds with a strong affirmation of the Church's historic faith. Jesus is, in the words of the apostle Thomas, "My Lord and my God!" (John 20:28).

Regarding *discipleship*, the life of the Presbyterian Church (U.S.A.) has been rocked by divisive conflicts over the nature and character of the Christian life, particularly in the realm of sexual ethics. Central to these debates has been the question of the Church's relationship to the surrounding culture, with the suggestion frequently arising that the Church must adapt and accommodate its teaching to the values and mores of secular society. The Declaration seeks to respond with a strong affirmation of the Church's historic teaching that Christian discipleship means a *transformed or amended life* in light of the revelation of God in Christ. As Paul put it, "Do not be conformed to this world, but be transformed by the renewing of your minds" (Rom. 12:2).

Regarding *authority*, the life and mission of the Presbyterian Church (U.S.A.) has been hampered by the erosion of biblical authority within its common life and by the breakdown of any sort of working consensus on how the Bible is to be interpreted—the so-called hermeneutical question. The Declaration makes a clear affirmation of the authority of Scripture and establishes a theological framework within which radically divergent interpretations of the Bible can be faithfully sorted out in a manner consistent with Christ's promise to the Church of the gift of the Holy Spirit who will "guide you into all the truth" (John 16:13).

Regarding *mission*, the dramatic decline in PC(USA) membership over recent decades has received widespread attention. This decline has been accompanied by a growing hesitancy in some quarters to share the Gospel of Jesus Christ with people who have not yet heard or accepted the Good News. The Declaration responds with a clear affirmation of the *missional nature of the Church*. It presents an understanding of the Church as the continuation of Christ's own mission to seek and save the lost: "Go therefore and make disciples of all nations . . ." (Matt. 28:19).

Finally, regarding *Church unity*, the question confronting the Presbyterian Church (U.S.A.) in these days is whether there is anything in its life or faith capable of uniting its diverse and oftentimes quarreling constituencies. Our Church finds itself in the waning days of a failed experiment that tried to hold together the Church's life and mission without a clear consensus on the foundations of our life together. Presbyterians earlier in this century thought they could establish harmony by setting aside fundamental questions of theology, rallying instead around a common commitment to "mission, mission, mission." That hope has been discredited as we have come to recognize that the character of mission is decisively shaped by the faith that undergirds it. Theology matters. It cannot simply be set aside. The Declaration grows out of the conviction that there is only one foundation capable of sustaining the Church's life and unity—Jesus Christ, the Son of God, as he is presented in the Scriptures and confessed by faithful Christians through the ages under the guidance of the Holy Spirit. Our unity, when it comes, is not the product of regarding all views equally, as if the choice between them did not matter. It is the gift of "one Lord, one faith, one baptism, one God and Father of all" that is ours in the Gospel (Eph. 4:5–6).

The Central Theme of the Declaration

How do we tie these various concerns together? To do this, the Declaration employs the classical Reformed or Calvinist doctrine of mystical (or spiritual) union of the believer with Christ. (The traditional Latin name for this doctrine is the *Unio mystica cum Christo*.) At the very beginning of his discussion of the Christian life in *Institutes of the Christian Religion*, John

Calvin asks how the things that Christ has accomplished come to have any relevance for us. His conclusion:

> First, we must understand that as long as Christ remains outside of us, and we are separated from him, all that he has suffered and done for the salvation of the human race remains useless and of no value for us. Therefore, to share with us what he has received from the Father, he had to become ours and to dwell within us.[1]

In order for Christ's benefits to have any meaning or application for us, we must be united with him and he with us.

> Therefore, that joining together of Head and members, that indwelling of Christ in our hearts—in short, that mystical union—are accorded by us the highest degree of importance, so that Christ, having been made ours, makes us sharers with him in the gifts with which he has been endowed.[2]

This union of the believer with Christ is a work of the Holy Spirit.

Here in this doctrine of the believer's union with Christ in the power of the Spirit we find the thread that is capable of tying together our confession of Christ (Christology) with our understandings of discipleship, authority, mission, and Church unity (see discussion on pp. 3–5). As the Holy Spirit unites believers with Jesus Christ, our discipleship becomes an expression and an outgrowth of his life within us: "It is no longer I who live, but it is Christ who lives in me" (Gal. 2:20). Our approach to Scripture finds its anchor in Christ's own knowledge of the Father: " 'For who has known the mind of the Lord so as to instruct him?' But we have the mind of Christ" (1 Cor. 2:16). Our mission becomes a participation in and extension of his mission: "As the Father has sent me, even so I send you" (John 20:21). Our unity with one another emerges as the product of our all being joined together in union with him: "So we, who are many, are

---

1. John Calvin, *Institutes of the Christian Religion*, edited by John T. McNeil and translated by Ford Lewis Battles (Philadelphia: The Westminster Press, 1960), III.i.1.

2. Ibid., III.xi.10.

Union in Christ

one body in Christ, and individually we are members one of another" (Rom. 12:5).

The structure of the Declaration reflects the development of this theme. It begins with a confession of Christ, establishing its christological foundations in section I. Next, section II sets forth a description of the way our union with Christ comes about by the work of the Holy Spirit in the Church's ministry of Word and Sacrament. Sections III, IV, and V then embark on an exploration of the implications of our union with Christ for the discipleship, mission, and unity of Christian believers within the Church.

The Church's life of faith in response to the love of God the Father takes place in our union with Christ the Son by the power of the Holy Spirit. The theological roots of the Declaration are thus solidly Trinitarian. Contrary to popular misconceptions, the doctrine of the Trinity is not an abstract set of mathematical or philosophical puzzles over how one could equal three could equal one. Rather, the doctrine of the Trinity is a thoroughly biblical understanding of God that is determined never to conceive of God apart from God's own self-revelation as Father, Son, and Holy Spirit. The Christian life, as set forth by the Declaration, is through and through the work in us of this Trinitarian God. In and through Christ, men and women enter into his knowledge of and communion with the Father ("Whoever has seen me has seen the Father" [John 14:9]). In and through Christ, men and women share in his mission from the Father for the sake of the world. In the shorthand formulation of classical Trinitarian theology, we affirm that the whole of the Christian life is a process of our coming to the Father, through the Son, in the Holy Spirit, and of our sharing through the same Spirit in the life and ministry of the Son given from the Father.

For Reflection and Discussion

1. What conditions in Church and culture occasion the writing of *Union in Christ: A Declaration for the Church*? Rank them in order of importance to you.

2. Consider the difference between a declaration and a confession. How does each benefit the Church? In what way does a declaration (or confession) encourage or discourage personal theological formation?

3. Why is Christ's question "Who do you say that I am?" so relevant to life today? What other questions are especially relevant today?

Confessing Jesus Christ

The Title and Opening Affirmation

"Union in Christ: A Declaration for the Church"

The church has union in Christ because we have union with Christ. This classical Christian understanding of the life of faith was specifically employed by John Calvin. Because we are grafted into Christ, or joined to him, which is the work of the Holy Spirit, we participate in his own relationship with and mission from the Father. The whole of Christian faith and life flows from this idea, which is the basis for the unity of the church.

Union with Christ is a theological concept with a long history of use in the Church. More important, however, is the way of life to which it refers. Those baptized into Christ are united with him into a spiritual relationship that now defines them in their core identity. We mean this not just in a psychological sense, by which we understand ourselves as

Christians, but even more deeply in the sense that our fundamental constitution as persons is formed by our union with Christ. The writer to the Ephesians calls this a "new self" (Eph. 4:24). It is the result of our being "born from above" by the power of the Holy Spirit (John 3:3). By our union with Christ we are "a new creation" (2 Cor. 5:17), enabled to put aside our false selves and to live as free persons, as true selves.

He is before all things, and in him all things hold together.

The opening affirmation cites Col. 1:17. Jesus Christ is Lord of all, from beginning to end! And outside of him everything disintegrates. Separated from this center, human life begins to lapse back into chaos and nonbeing. Above all else, the Declaration affirms the centrality of Paul's conviction that the Christian life is life "in Christ" (e.g., 2 Cor. 5:17–21; Gal. 3:15–21).

Finally, in the opening affirmation there is the claim that what follows is a restatement of the biblical, historical faith of the Church. To repeat: this is not "new" theology (mindful of the warning in Eph. 4:14, lest we be "children, tossed to and fro and blown about by every wind of doctrine"). The intent is to express the faith that has sustained the Church through the ages, in contemporary images and in such a manner that significant problems in our life together are purposefully addressed.

Confessing Christ

Jesus Christ is the gracious mission of God to the world and for the world.

The Declaration begins with the words "Jesus Christ," and not with our own faith or the institutional Church. Much modern theology, both so-called evangelical and liberal, tends to begin with our own experience. Theology comes to be defined, then, as reflection on experience. The theology of the Declaration moves in a different direction. It is a reflection on Jesus Christ, in whose risen and ascended life we share through the Holy Spirit. He is the center of faith and life, not we ourselves. It is in union with him, in fact, that we discover our true identity.

Jesus Christ is the gracious mission of God.

This is not an immediately familiar description of Jesus, but with the rest of the opening paragraph it defines and confesses who Jesus is. It emphasizes that we can only know the meaning of his work as Savior when we know who he is as Son of the Father. Jesus is the purpose of God: "I do as the Father has commanded me" (John 14:31). He comes with a job to do. That is his work.

Some might question why we need to proclaim that Jesus is the mission of God. Wouldn't saying that Jesus "embodies" or "carries out" the mission of God to the world and for the world be a more natural way of putting it? But to say that Jesus Christ "embodied" the mission of God would imply that such a mission was a separate entity, standing potentially on its own apart from the particular person known to us as Jesus of Nazareth. This would introduce the possibility that other historical figures or movements (Mohammed, Buddha, or the Labor Movement, for example) might also embody or carry forward this abstract entity now called "the mission of God." As a safeguard against such abstractions, the Declaration affirms that Jesus *is* God's mission to the world and for the world. With this statement the Declaration makes it crystal clear that there is simply no talking about God's mission to the world apart from the historical figure of Jesus of Nazareth.

Jesus thus comes not just as a messenger of God—not simply a prophet like Isaiah or Jeremiah or John the Baptist. He comes as *Emmanuel,* as God with us in human flesh, God in our midst as a particular human being. In the fourth century, the Church codified this central affirmation of faith in the Nicene Creed's assertion that Jesus is "of one substance with the Father." Jesus in the flesh is "God incarnate as Mary's son," God among us as Jesus. This is the core faith of the Church.

His coming is "the gracious mission of God." It is a gracious coming because he comes as God for us, to do for us in the flesh of our humanity what must be done to restore us to union and communion with the Father. The whole doctrine of the atonement can be assumed here. So he comes not just as "Emmanuel," but as "Emmanuel *and Savior.*" He comes not just "to the world" but also "for the world."

As God with us and for us, Jesus nevertheless reveals what it means to be *the truly human one.* As *Lord of all,* in the union of his divinity and humanity, he also totally remakes human nature to be now fully conformed to the image of God. He is thus "the firstborn of all creation" (Col. 1:15). In Jesus we see what a human being was intended to be in the purposes of God. We Christians confess therefore that we only discover and live the fullness of our humanity when we live in union with Christ, the truly human One.

His coming transforms everything. . . .

If God has come to us as a particular human being, everything has changed. The following five sentences unpack what that means.

First, his authority is primary. *His Lordship casts down every idolatrous claim to authority.* There is no power in the world, no regime, no religious or political authority, no economic order, no worldly dominion that stands above Jesus Christ and his Lordship. None can claim from us a loyalty that supersedes or contradicts our loyalty to Christ. With this affirmation the Declaration echoes the central theme of the *Theological Declaration of Barmen*: "Jesus Christ, as he is attested for us in Holy Scripture, is the one Word of God which we have to hear and which we have to trust and obey in life and in death" (*BOC*, 8.11).

The primacy of Jesus means—to be clear about this—that other authorities are not primary. We are not primary. The Church is not primary. Not even the Bible is primary. That does not mean that we, the Church, and the Bible are not authorities in their appropriate sense. The Bible, for example, is authoritative precisely because it provides unique and authentic testimony to Christ. But we, the Church, and the Bible serve Jesus Christ, "that at the name of Jesus every knee should bend, in heaven and on earth and under the earth, and every tongue confess that Jesus Christ is Lord, to the glory of God the Father" (Phil. 2:10–11).

Second, *His incarnation discloses the only path to God.* The Declaration takes John 14:6 very seriously: "No one comes to the Father except through me." This is both an absolute claim and a singular statement of authority. In the face of today's religious pluralism, this affirmation may well strike an offensive note. While we should respect all religious viewpoints, and certainly treat all persons of whatever creed with dignity, Christian faith as expressed by the Declaration makes a singular claim for Jesus Christ. He alone is the Mediator who reveals the Father and does God's work, and who brings us home to the Father in union with himself. All other paths to God are inadequate. This claim, it should be noted, is not made on behalf of the Church, or any theological school, but is made on behalf of Jesus Christ, who makes it for himself.

Certain persons might object here that some knowledge about God does come to us on occasion through our experience of God's works in the created order. The Apostle Paul makes the claim that "ever since the creation of the world his eternal power and divine nature, invisible though they are, have been understood and seen through the things he has made" (Rom. 1:20). Lesslie Newbigin, a distinguished missionary and bishop of the Church of South India, tells about bringing the Gospel for the first time to natives of a remote tribal village. Their joyous response to the proclamation of the Good News: "We had always hoped God was like that!" Missionaries frequently have the sense, reports Newbigin, that the Holy Spirit has preceded them, preparing the way for the Gospel through the general religious experience and apprehensions of people who have not yet heard about Jesus.

In confessing Jesus' incarnation as the only path to God, we do not deny the existence of these confused and partial intimations of God. We are confessing, however, that such intimations are no substitute for the saving proclamation of the Gospel, and that in Christ we encounter the definitive revelation of God by which we are able to sort out truth from falsehood in these other dim and partial apprehensions. Calvin paints a vivid picture of the way the biblical testimony to Christ serves to clarify and sort out the blurred confusion of prior intimations of God:

Just as old or bleary-eyed men and those with weak vision, if you thrust before them a most beautiful volume, even if they recognize it to be some sort of writing, yet can scarcely construe two words, but with the aid of spectacles will begin to read distinctly; so Scripture, gathering up the otherwise confused knowledge of God in our minds, having dispersed our dullness, clearly shows us the true God.[1]

Third, *His life shows what it means to be human*. We have already made some mention of this above. The emphasis here, however, is on the power of his life to reveal human being in its fullness. His love, purposeful ministry, relationships, and God-centeredness show what being human involves. This stands over and against the claims of many merchants of self-fulfillment in our culture. True humanity is not found in the accumulation of wealth or acquisitiveness, in power, or in self-indulgence, but in Jesus Christ. As the medieval monastics well knew, the really spiritual enemies were to be dealt with through their vows of poverty, chastity, and obedience. In contemporary terms, our union with Christ leads us to confront the accommodations we have made to money, sex, and power.

On yet another level, we can say that our own deepest identity as human beings is found in union with Christ, who is the truly human One. Who we are is not defined by our achievements, possessions, personality, or natural endowments but by the fact that God has been gracious to us and become one with us in Jesus Christ. As we are united with Christ, we find our own authentic humanity. One result of this union of believers *with* Christ is their union with one another *in* Christ. By this union the Church finds authority in community.

Fourth, *His atoning death reveals the depth of God's love for sinners*. The Gospel is about the love of God. Far too often, perhaps, we have placed law before love, or made the love of God conditional on our own acts. The atonement is not the condition for but the consequence of the love of God.

---

1. John Calvin, *Institutes of the Christian Religion*, edited by John T. McNeil and translated by Ford Lewis Battles (Philadelphia: The Westminster Press, 1960), I.vi.1.

"God so loved the world . . ." (John 3:16). The gospel of the love of God is prior to our response (gratitude). It is God's forgiveness that conditions our repentance, God's grace that calls for our obedience, and God's love that enables our faithfulness.

Fifth, *His bodily resurrection shatters the powers of sin and death*. Evil and death, rife in our world, do not have the last word. Life conquers death in the resurrection. Evil is vanquished. Even hell itself cannot hold the Lord of life, for he rose again on the third day. The resurrection of Christ is a bodily resurrection. This is a great mystery. What we refer to is spiritual, to be sure, for the resurrected body is a *spiritual* body. But because it is the resurrection of the *body*, a future for the material life we live on earth exists. In the continuity between Christ's earthly body of flesh and blood and his glorious, resurrected body, we discern that God's final plan is not to discard and abandon this creation, but to renew and perfect and redeem it in glory. For this reason among others, Christians take creation seriously. In union with Christ, we, in the wholeness of our personhoods, anticipate in hope the new life in communion with God.

For Reflection and Discussion

1. Discuss the very strong assertion that the whole of Christian faith and life flows from our union in Christ. Express in your own words how you understand the meaning of union in Christ. Then look at some of the following Pauline uses of "in Christ":

   Rom. 3:24; 6:11, 23; 8:1–2; 12:5; 16:9–10

   1 Cor. 1:2, 4, 30; 15:22

   2 Cor. 2:14; 5:17, 19

   Gal. 2:4; 3:26, 28; 5:6

   Eph. 2:13

   (There are many more such usages. See also "in him," and "in the Lord.")

2. The Declaration begins with an affirmation of historical connectedness to emphasize that it is not inventing a new theology. Reflect on what it means for us to be part of a communion of faith linked with the Church through the ages.

3. The first words are "Jesus Christ." Why?

4. The phrase "Jesus Christ is the gracious mission of God . . ." states in a few words the meaning of the incarnation and the atonement. Discuss this idea. How does it help clarify the content of Christian faith and living?

5. Discuss the five defining aspects of the *person* of Jesus Christ ("Emmanuel and Savior"; "one with the Father"; "God incarnate as Mary's Son"; "Lord of all"; "The truly human one"). What does each of these say about Jesus Christ? Why is that important? What would you add or delete?

6. Following the statement "His coming transforms everything" are five assertions that refer to the *work* of Jesus Christ (pp. 12–15). Explore how each assertion develops the transforming aspect of the gospel.

The Work of the Trinity in the Life of the Church

Overview

The Holy Spirit joins us to Jesus Christ by grace alone, uniting our life with his through the ministry of the Church.

This section introduces the major theme that links the confession of Christ in section I to the practical concerns of the Declaration. That theme is the union of believers with Jesus Christ by the power of the Holy Spirit.

Even in biblical times, not everyone who heard or saw Jesus came to faith in him. The New Testament preserves the memory that some who were eyewitnesses to Jesus' ministry thought he was possessed by the devil (Mark 3:22). The same is true today: Not everyone who hears the gospel of Christ—however skillfully proclaimed—recognizes Christ as the Word of God and believes. It is not enough just to hear about Jesus or, even like those first witnesses, to see him face to face. Something extra is required for us to recognize and respond to him as the Son of God. That "extra" is the work of the Holy Spirit, who opens our eyes so we may recognize Jesus and believe. As Jesus tells Nicodemus in John 3, unless a person is born anew by water and the Spirit, he or she can neither recognize nor enter the Kingdom of God. "No one can say 'Jesus is Lord' except by the Holy Spirit" (1 Cor. 12:3b).

But the New Testament also describes this work of the Holy Spirit in terms much stronger than simply having our eyes opened or receiving a certain type of knowledge. The Spirit *engrafts us into Christ* (Rom. 11:17), so that we become members of his Body (1 Cor. 12:12–13). Christians are persons who have "put on" Christ (Gal. 3:27). In Calvin's words, "The Holy Spirit is the bond by which Christ effectual unites us to himself."[1]

God bestows this gift of union with Christ through the Holy Spirit by the operations of what are called the "ordinary means of grace"—the Church's ministry of Word and Sacrament. Through these ordinances and activities of the Church, God brings people to faith and nurtures them in their union with Christ. This is not to say that God does not sometimes bring people to Christ through extraordinary means—a foxhole experience in a war, for instance, or a near-death experience or a profoundly affecting dream or vision. In Karl Barth's colorful observation, "God may speak to us through Russian Communism, a flute concerto, a blossoming shrub, or a dead dog."[2] But in the ordinary course of things, God has provided us with the Church's ministry of Word and Sacrament as the regular means through which the Spirit unites us with Christ. It is the implications of that work of the Spirit within the Church that constitute the focus of this section of the Declaration.

---

1. John Calvin, *Institutes of the Christian Religion*, edited by John T. McNeil and translated by Ford Lewis Battles (Philadelphia: The Westminster Press, 1960), III.i.1

2. Karl Barth, *Church Dogmatics: The Doctrine of the Word of God*, vol. 1 (Edinburgh: T. & T. Clark, 1975), p. 55.

Union in Christ

The Ministry of the Word

In the proclamation of the Word, the Spirit calls us to repentance, builds up and renews our life in Christ, strengthens our faith, empowers our service, gladdens our hearts, and transforms our lives more fully into the image of Christ.

The Word of God is different from human words. Human words are often empty, conveying falsehoods, hollow promises, idle dreams. God's Word, by contrast, is powerful and truthful: "It shall not return to me empty, but it shall accomplish that which I purpose, and succeed in the thing for which I sent it" (Isa 55:11). Think of God *speaking* the whole universe into existence in Genesis 1, or Jesus stilling the storm or raising the dead with his authoritative Word (Matt. 8:26–27; Mark 5:41–42)! God's Word *does* things. It is full of power.

And this Word of God, with all its life-transforming power, is active in and through the ministry of the Church. As the *Second Helvetic Confession* so boldly puts it, "the preaching of the Word of God *is* the Word of God" (*BOC*, 5.004). It is through the power of this Word that the Holy Spirit strengthens and renews our life in Christ, sustaining our union with him. This paragraph of the Declaration does not give a chronological description of the conversion process but rather suggests different ways that God's Word affects human hearts and lives.

We turn away from forms of Church life that ignore the need for repentance, that discount the transforming power of the Gospel, or that fail to pray, hope, and strive for a life that is pleasing to God.

As we affirm and celebrate what the gospel is, we necessarily also reject those things that are contrary to it. This paragraph is the first of eleven scattered throughout the Declaration that point to false forms of discipleship ruled out by our acceptance of the gospel. The language of these statements ("We turn away from forms of Church life . . .") is intended to be modest. It intentionally avoids any hint of self-righteous holiness or looking down one's nose at all those *other* sinners. The language directs the reader not to what others are doing or not doing but to what *we* intend to do—those of us who embrace the Good News to which the Declaration points.

In particular, this paragraph turns us away from understandings of discipleship that deny the power of the Word. We here reject a Christianity that acts as though people could be recipients of the Holy Spirit's ministry, held and sustained in union with Christ, without being inwardly and outwardly affected by such an experience. One of the popular distortions of the gospel encountered these days is the claim that, in Christ, God accepts and affirms us "just the way we are." This is *partly* true. In the cross of Christ, God does reach out to sinners with unconditional love, grace, and acceptance. But the *purpose* and *result* of God's reaching out in this way is our engrafting into Christ by the power of the Spirit, so that we may begin the long, slow process of healing, of growing up into the image of Christ.

The Declaration does not here assume that such healing will be complete in this lifetime. It speaks not of perfect obedience or faultless perfection but of praying, hoping, and striving for a life that is pleasing to God. It is such a life as Paul described:

> Not that I have already obtained this or have already
> reached the goal; but I press on to make it my own, because
> Christ Jesus has made me his own. Beloved, I do not
> consider that I have made it my own; but this one thing I do,
> forgetting what lies behind and straining forward to what lies
> ahead, I press on toward the goal for the prize of the
> heavenly call of God in Christ Jesus. (Phil. 3:12–14)

A gospel that did not result in this straining forward, in this eager longing for the prize of God's upward call in Christ Jesus, would be nothing but a tragic and hopeless resignation to the power of our own sinfulness. It is this false gospel that we rule out when we recognize and embrace the working of the triune God—Father, Son, and Holy Spirit—in and through the Church's ministry of proclamation.

Baptism

In Baptism and conversion the Spirit engrafts us into Christ, establishing the Church's unity and binding us to one another in him.

Baptism marks our entrance into the community of faith and our engrafting into Christ by the Holy Spirit. Baptism has classically been described in the Reformed tradition as a "sign and seal" of our union with Christ. This language can be a bit misleading. Modern people usually think of a sign as an empty vessel—a sort of placeholder pointing to realities that are not immediately present. But when Calvin and the writers of our *Book of Confessions* speak about a sign, they have in mind something very different. In their understanding, sacraments are signs that genuinely *make present* what they signify.

This understanding becomes clearer when we think carefully about what a "seal" is. A *seal* was the distinctive impression made by the signet ring of a monarch, affixed to a document to show that it was an official proclamation of the throne. A modern-day equivalent would be the signature of a president or governor affixed to a piece of legislation. Such a seal or signature is a sign of a leader's authority, but it is a sign that makes present what it signifies. The presidential signature on a piece of legislation is precisely what confers authority to it, making it the law of the land. Extending the analogy to baptism, we could say that the gospel promises of our engrafting into Christ and our resulting adoption as children of God form the "text" of the divine legislation offered on our behalf. The Sacrament of Baptism then comprises the "signature" of God, visible to faith, that confers authority and surety to these promises.

This "strong" understanding of baptism as more than a mere sign receives an especially forthright statement in the *Scots Confession:*

> These sacraments . . . were instituted by God not only to
> make a visible distinction between his people and those who
> were without the Covenant [i.e., by admitting them to
> Church membership], but also to exercise the faith of his

children and, by participation of these sacraments, to seal in their hearts the assurance of his promise, and of that most blessed conjunction, union, and society, which the chosen have with their Head, Christ Jesus. And so we utterly condemn the vanity of those who affirm the sacraments to be nothing else than naked and bare signs. No, we assuredly believe that by Baptism we are engrafted into Christ Jesus, to be made partakers of his righteousness, by which our sins are covered and remitted, and also that in the Supper rightly used, Christ Jesus is so joined with us that he becomes the very nourishment and food of our souls. (*BOC*, 3.21)

The Scots Confession here reflects New Testament affirmations that we are baptized "into" Christ (Rom. 6:3); that all who are baptized have "clothed [themselves] with" Christ (Gal. 3:27); that by one Spirit we have all been baptized into one body of Christ (1 Cor. 12:12–13).

If that is true, what do we make of people who are baptized as infants and reject the faith later in life? Are they automatically engrafted into Christ and saved, apart from any active faith or commitment of their own? Assuredly not. The Declaration here specifies that our engrafting into Christ takes place by "Baptism *and conversion*," thus emphasizing that our baptism into Christ is inseparable from the life of faith that lays active claim to God's promises. For the person baptized as an infant, we affirm with the *Scots Confession* and the New Testament that such a person has been genuinely joined and united with Christ. But that engrafting is completed and fulfilled only by the person's conversion as he or she reaches an age of discernment later in life. Engrafting into Christ is inseparable from life in Christ. Faith and discipleship in later life—even if the person has fallen away for a significant period of time—are the outworking and fulfillment of the union with Christ that was sealed in that person's Baptism as an infant. In Calvin's words, "Infants are baptized into future repentance and faith, and even though these have not yet been formed in them, the seed of both lies hidden within them by the secret working of the Spirit."[2]

2. Ibid., IV.x.vi.20.

What then do we say of persons who are baptized as children and fall away, never to return to the Church? What has become of their baptismal engrafting into Christ? Are we saying that baptism provides them an automatic assurance of salvation, no matter what? Calvin's treatment of this question is instructive. While the grace and promise of our engrafting into Christ is genuinely offered to us in baptism, he says, that grace can be rejected by the stubborn and sinful human hearts of persons who have reached the age of discernment. Speaking of his own life and conversion, Calvin says,

> We indeed, being blind and unbelieving, for a long time did not grasp the promise that had been given us in baptism; yet that promise, since it was of God, ever remained fixed and firm and trustworthy. Even if all men are liars and faithless, still God does not cease to be trustworthy [Rom. 3:3]. Even if all men are lost, still Christ remains salvation. We therefore confess that for that time baptism benefitted us not at all, inasmuch as the promise offered us in it—without which baptism is nothing—lay neglected.[3]

Calvin's argument is echoed by the *Second Helvetic Confession:*

> So the Sacraments, which by the Word consist of signs and the things signified, remain true and inviolate Sacraments, signifying not only sacred things, but, by God offering, the things signified, even if unbelievers do not receive the things offered. This is not the fault of God who gives and offers them, but the fault of men who receive them without faith and illegitimately; but whose unbelief does not invalidate the faithfulness of God. (*BOC*, 5.183)

The apostle Paul, who placed great emphasis on baptism as an act that unites us with Christ, also used Old Testament examples to warn his churches against relying on this grace of the sacraments as something automatic, as though this gift of God did not have to be accepted by faith and a life of genuine discipleship (1 Cor. 10:1ff.). The grace of our

---

3. Ibid., IV.xv.17.

promised engrafting into Christ is genuinely held out to all who receive the sacrament; but that grace can be rejected by sinful hearts that stubbornly turn away from the love and generosity of God.

If the Sacrament of Baptism unites all of us to Christ, it also unites us *with one another* in him. We who have been baptized are all one body, with Christ as the head (Rom. 12:4–5; Eph. 4:4–6). The foundation of the Church's unity therefore comes to us as a gift from Christ, as the Spirit engrafts us together into him.

We turn away from forms of Church life that seek unity in theological pluralism, relativism, or syncretism.

If the Church's unity is established *in Christ*, that rules out other possible foundations for unity, many of which have been tried and found wanting in the recent history of the Presbyterian Church. We might, for instance, declare that all religious beliefs are equally valid and equally deserving of acceptance within the Church. Further, we might say that this "inclusive" kind of attitude, which accepts any and all religious beliefs, is what should hold our life together as a Church. To do so would be to embrace *theological pluralism* as the heart of the Church's unity. Such a view places a particular kind of open-mindedness, rather than devotion to Jesus, at the center of the Church's life. (Ironically, some "open-minded" people condemn and exclude others who are not "inclusive" and "tolerant" and "open-minded" in the same way they are!) One must distinguish theological pluralism, which accepts any and all religious beliefs as equally valid, from *cultural pluralism*, which welcomes people from a wide variety of cultural backgrounds into the life of the Church, affirming the value of the particular gifts each one brings. Cultural pluralism within the Church can be a powerful expression of the unity that the Holy Spirit gives us across all the cultural, ethnic, and national boundaries that might otherwise separate us. As such, cultural pluralism is fully compatible with the Christ-centered faith that the Declaration lifts up, whereas theological pluralism is not.

A similar position is that of *religious relativism*, which denies that there is any overarching truth about God, the world, and human beings that might command our common loyalty and serve as the basis of our life together in the Church. From a relativistic perspective, the only "truth" available is that which one has decided will be true *for oneself*. Personal preferences and choices are all one has. Thus religious convictions in this view are not a response to God's living presence breaking into the world and human lives but a set of arbitrary symbols chosen to express an individual's personal religious feelings. A unity based on this sort of relativism would simply regard all religious beliefs and perspectives as equally acceptable for the Church, since no particular belief could be said to be more truthful than any other.

Religious syncretism seeks a somewhat different path to Church unity. Syncretism combines elements of different religious faiths into a hybrid blend that contains elements of each. An example of this would be Israel's blending of orthodox Yahweh-worship and Canaanite Baal religions—a hybrid faith that was hotly condemned by the Old Testament prophets. Syncretism seeks unity among a variety of religious beliefs by producing a religious life and worship that contains "something for everyone."

Over against these rather dubious strategies for holding together different religious loyalties within a single religious community, the Declaration declares that the Church's unity is the product of our baptismal engrafting into the one Body of Christ by the power of the Holy Spirit. Only Jesus Christ has the power to hold together the Christian community in the face of the many forces that threaten to divide it. Our unity will be in him if it is to be at all.

The Lord's Supper

In the Lord's Supper the Spirit nurtures and nourishes our participation in Christ and our communion with one another in him.

If Baptism is the sign and seal of our engrafting into Christ, the Lord's Supper is the sign and seal of the Spirit's nourishing us in that union, through our spiritual feeding on the body and blood of Christ. As the *Scots Confession* puts it, "Thus we confess and believe without doubt that the faithful, in the right use of the Lord's Table, do so eat the body and drink the blood of the Lord Jesus that he remains in them and they in him" (*BOC*, 3.21).

Calvin calls this union with Christ the "special fruit" of the Lord's Supper, which results in the assurance both of salvation and of forgiveness of sins:

> Godly souls can gather great assurance and delight from this Sacrament; in it they have a witness of our growth into one body with Christ such that whatever is his may be called ours. As a consequence, we may dare assure ourselves that eternal life, of which he is the heir, is ours; and that the Kingdom of Heaven, into which he has already entered, can no more be cut off from us than from him; again, that we cannot be condemned for our sins, from whose guilt he has absolved us, since he willed to take them upon himself as if they were his own.[4]

In a similar vein, Martin Luther compared this union with Christ to a marriage between Christ the bridegroom and the soul of the believer, which is his bride. Though the comparison reflects sixteenth-century marriage customs, the analogy is still a powerful one. The bride brings to this marriage a dowry, says Luther, consisting of all the soul's sins. These become the property of Christ the bridegroom and no longer belong to the believer. In exchange, the bride in this union comes to share in all her husband's property, that is, in all of Christ's righteousness. So our union with Christ, nourished and nurtured in the Lord's Supper, becomes foundational to our belief in the forgiveness of sins.

---

4. Ibid., IV.xvii.2.

We turn away from forms of Church life that allow human divisions of race, gender, nationality, or economic class to mar the Eucharistic fellowship, as though in Christ there were still walls of separation dividing the human family.

The Declaration again in this paragraph focuses on the union of believers with one another that comes about as a result of their union with Christ. The discussion of baptism held up union with Christ as the sole foundation of our unity in the Christian community, in opposition to rival means of trying to bind the Church together. Here in its consideration of the Lord's Supper, the Declaration confesses that the union in Christ that is given to the Eucharistic fellowship (i.e., the community of persons who rightly partake of the Lord's Supper together) is a stronger force than all of the human factors that work to divide people. "There is no longer Jew or Greek, there is no longer slave or free, there is no longer male or female; for all of you are one in Christ Jesus" (Gal. 3:28).

For this reason the Church cannot allow human divisions of race, class, gender, and nationality to define the character of its own life. In Christ, these divisions have been overcome. This recognition serves to affirm the Church's historic stands against injustice and discrimination. It might also caution us against the dangers of hardening human divisions into fixed and permanent quota systems for representation within the organizations of the Church, as if the raising up of leaders in the Church were a matter of mechanically fulfilling formulas rather than discerning the gifts of the Spirit.

For Reflection and Discussion

1. Reflect on and discuss why the work of the Holy Spirit is important in accomplishing our union in Christ.

2. What are the "ordinary means of grace," and what is "ordinary" about them?

3. Discuss the importance of the proclamation of the Word of God in the ministry of the Church. What does this suggest about how a minister should spend his or her time throughout the week? How much time does your session and congregation expect your minister to spend in study and sermon preparation?

4. The Declaration lists eleven things Christians should avoid (the statements that begin "we turn away from . . .") . Evaluate each of these. What cultural and ecclesiastical conditions have made these statements of Christian intent (these are not mere condemnations) necessary?

5. Discuss the tension between God accepting us "just as we are" and God calling us to live an amended life. Are there certain times in the Church's life where one side of this tension should be emphasized over the other? If so, when?

6. The relationship between baptism and conversion is notoriously difficult to explain. Reflect on the position offered by the Declaration and interpreted in the commentary.

7. The Declaration turns away from forms of Church life that seek unity "in theological pluralism, relativism, or syncretism." This may appear to some to be a "hard line" position. Why does the interpretation of unity

in Christ in the commentary lead to the rejection of other suggested bases for unity? What do you understand "unity in Christ" to mean?

8. Why does the Church not allow divisions of race, gender, nationality, or economic class into the eucharistic fellowship? How true is this in your local congregation?

Our Life in Christ

Overview

Engrafted into Jesus Christ we participate through faith in his relationship with the Father.

Running through the Declaration is the theology of Heb. 3:1, where we read that Jesus Christ is the Apostle and High Priest of our confession. He is the true and sole Mediator between God and creation. As the Son of the Father, bearing always the flesh of our humanity, he brings God to us and us to God. Bringing God to us, he is the true Apostle, the true Word of God. He comes not just revealing something about God, but God himself in saving atonement in the humanity of his personhood as the bearer of our sin. Bringing us to God, he is our High Priest, leading us to share both in his own relationship with the Father and in his mission from the Father, for the sake of the world. In this section the Declaration spells out three implications of the priestly ministry of Christ by which he gives us to share in what is his: his righteousness before God, his knowledge of the Father, and his love of the Father.

There is an ancient theological axiom that goes back to St. Athanasius in the fourth century: Christ became human that we might be made divine.[1] By this, the great Egyptian Church father intended that by virtue of the incarnation and the atonement, God in Christ has acted on us in such a way that we are united with Christ, partaking of him, to share thereby in his own intimacy with the Father. This does not mean that we become gods; it does mean that, united with Christ, we share in his own life in God, in this case, his righteousness, his knowledge, and his love. By this sharing, the things that are his become ours by grace.

Addressing God as 'Father'

It is perhaps necessary now to say something about the use of the word *Father* for God, found most markedly in this section of the Declaration. The center of the New Testament is the relationship between Jesus Christ and the One he addresses as Father. The communion between Jesus and his heavenly Father is an utterly unique relationship, of which we can know nothing apart from Jesus' own testimony.

God is thus Father not by comparison to human fathers, but *only* in the Trinitarian relation, as Father of the Son. Whenever *Father* is used of God it means "the One whom Jesus called Father." The paradigm text is John 1:18: "No one has ever seen God. It is God the only Son, who is close to the Father's heart, who has made him known." In Greek, the word for "made him known" is *exegesato*. Jesus "exegetes" or "interprets" the Father. The term does not denote a generic title for God outside of the Father-Son relationship. *Father* thus functions in Trinitarian language not as a descriptive metaphor but as a proper name, whose home is the relationship that exists from all eternity between the first and second Persons of the Trinity. That is a relationship to which we as creatures have no immediate knowledge or access.

But by an astonishing gift of grace, Jesus invites us to be united with himself in the power of the Holy Spirit, so that in union with him we

---

1. See *St. Athanasius, On the Incarnation* (Crestwood, NY: St. Vladimir's Seminary Press, 1993).

Union in Christ

may come to share in his utterly unique relation of Sonship to the Father. By ourselves we have absolutely no right or ground to address God as "Father." It is only as we are united with Christ, partaking of his communion with the Father, that we can truthfully address God in this way ourselves. In Paul's words,

> For all who are led by the Spirit of God are children of God.
> . . . When we cry, "Abba! Father!" it is that very Spirit
> bearing witness with our spirit that we are children of God,
> and if children, then heirs, heirs of God and joint heirs with
> Christ. (Rom. 8:14–17)

We know God only in and through Christ's relationship of Sonship, into which he invites us as participants ("Pray then like this: Our Father, who art in heaven . . ."). This means that salvation is understood as our communion *with* the Father *through* the Son *in the power of* the Holy Spirit. As Fanny Crosby's hymn put it, "O come to the Father through Jesus the Son, and give him the glory: great things he hath done!" Our knowledge of God and our hope for salvation are directly Trinitarian in their scope.

The traditional naming of the Trinitarian God as Father, Son, and Holy Spirit is sometimes replaced today by the functional titles of Creator, Redeemer, and Sustainer. This works as an occasional use, describing God's acts, but not as a substitute for the Trinitarian Name. The Fatherhood of God is tied utterly to Jesus' naming of his own relationship to God, into which relationship we, by the Spirit, participate.

It was St. Athanasius who noted that the only reason we have for calling God "Father" is that God is so named by Jesus in the Bible. This points to the historical shape that the Gospel took: Christian faith is a biblical faith and a Jesus-based faith. God's Fatherhood was understood relationally in and through Jesus Christ as self-giving love, and not as a human image or concept projected onto God. There is, in fact, an appropriate "thinking away" of that which is inappropriate in this terminology. By this we mean explicitly thinking away all biological and sexual imputation whatsoever into the theological concept of God. God the Father revealed in Scripture is Spirit. God has no sexual identity; sexuality, after all, is part of creation. The *imago Dei* (image of God) is not reversible; God is not created in our likeness! The personalized language of Trinitarian theology intends to bear witness in Christ to the liberation of humankind from all patriarchal idols and divinized ideologies. Where this did not and does not happen, there is a perversion of intent that must be utterly rejected on the ground of the nature and reference of Trinitarian language itself.

Sharing in Christ's Righteousness

By our union with Christ we participate in his righteousness before God, even as he becomes the bearer of our sin.

Righteousness is an abstract noun that really should be a verb! It means standing in a right relationship. It has a dynamic intention. Used of human beings, it means acting rightly before God, as in Matt. 5:6. Used of God, as, for example, in Rom. 3:5, it means the faithfulness or truthfulness of God. God keeps promises. It is also used of God in Rom. 3:25–26, to show that quality of holiness that not only condemns sin, but also, on the cross, decisively conquers sin. It is this latter image that the Declaration highlights. Together these examples may be taken to mean that God is true to who God is. The *Heidelberg Catechism* states that "God is indeed merciful and gracious, but he is also righteous. It is his righteousness which requires that sin committed against the supreme majesty of God be punished" (*BOC*, 4.011). The Catechism goes on immediately then to speak of our redemption in and through Jesus Christ "who is freely given to us for complete redemption and righteousness" (*BOC*, 4.018).

A guiding Scripture verse to consider is 2 Cor. 5:21: "For our sake [God] made him to be sin who knew no sin, so that in him we might become the righteousness of God." We cannot attain a right relationship with God by ourselves. We cannot stand before God in the strength of our own faith, piety, or good works. As difficult as that is for our religious and moral sensibilities to accept, this remains a cornerstone of evangelical theology. We who are sinners cannot redeem our own sin. We are truly helpless—maybe no more so than when we try to be religious! Self-righteousness is not righteousness before God. Only he who was not a sinner, yet was wholly human, God for us in and as Christ Jesus, could do for us what we could not do for ourselves. All that we can never be in the eyes of God, if we are left to ourselves, we become in Christ. Our sins are dealt with. That horrendous gulf that separates us from God because of our sin has been healed. Christ has borne our sins and thus they are borne away.

We are not now suddenly functionally perfected saints, of course. We still limp along, straining between sin and mercy, going on to perfection but very slowly indeed. Nevertheless, united with Christ we share in *his* right relationship with God. And that is very good news indeed.

We turn away from any claim to stand before God apart from Christ's own righteous obedience, manifest in his life and sacrifice for our sake on the cross.

Given the very nature of the gospel, that Christ died for our sins, the corollary is obviously true: we cannot stand before God *apart* from the saving life and death of Jesus Christ. Let us be very clear what this means. There is no way home to God—no salvation—outside of the person and work of Jesus. "Being of one substance with the Father . . . who for us men, and for our salvation, came down from heaven" (*BOC*, 1.2), Jesus is singularly the one through whom God "was pleased to reconcile to himself all things, whether on earth or in heaven, by making peace through the blood of his cross" (Col. 1:20).

Clearly the Declaration resists any attempt to dilute or diminish the work of the atonement. It is Jesus alone who is Savior. All the other claims to divinity and strategies pursued with a mind to union with God are rejected not just as worthless religious striving but also as sinful assertions of human disobedience in the face of the sole righteous obedience of Jesus Christ. It is not the Church in her arrogance who judges every attempt to be in relationship with God. The gospel is that Jesus Christ alone is Savior; in and through whom alone do we have access to the Father. This evangelical truth is the sole basis for evangelism. Reject it, and the whole message of the New Testament gets turned on its head. Try to engage in evangelism without it, and there is no point to the exercise.

Sharing in Christ's Knowledge

By our union with Christ we participate in his knowledge of the Father, given to us as the gift of faith through the unique and authoritative witness of the Old and New Testaments.

The Son knows the Father; the Father knows the Son. John's Gospel especially is replete with texts that affirm this. Chapters 14—17 build on the unity between the Father and the Son, coming to a climax at 17:26: "I made your name known to them." But the same theme appears in the other Gospels as well (e.g., Matt. 11:27: "All things have been handed over to me by my Father; and no one knows the Son except the Father, and no one knows the Father except the Son and any one to whom the Son chooses to reveal him.").

We can come to a knowledge of God in some regard through the book of nature. As Calvin intimated, nature is "the theater of God's glory." God is the creator, and God's creation carries the stamp of its maker. But as such, this is an inadequate knowledge of God. In particular, it is not a knowledge of God that knows God either as Savior or as Father, as one with whom we are in relationship. It is not a knowledge of God that can lead us to pray in union with Christ, "Our Father, who art in heaven, hallowed be Thy Name. . . ." St. Hilary of Poitiers (d. 367), a defender of Nicene orthodoxy and a theologian with a passion for knowledge of God, wrote that "the very center of saving faith is the belief not merely in God, but in God as Father, and not merely in Christ, but in Christ as Son of God."[2]

By our union with Christ we share in that intimate knowledge of the Father that is Christ's alone. True faith *is* a participation and a sharing in Christ's own knowledge of the Father, as we are united with him in the bond of the Spirit. As Paul puts it,

> The Spirit searches everything, even the depths of God. For what human being knows what is truly human except the human spirit that is within? So also no one comprehends what is truly God's except the Spirit of God. Now we have received not the spirit of the world, but the Spirit that is from God, so that we might understand the gifts bestowed on us by God. . . . "For who has known the mind of the Lord so as to instruct him?" But we have the mind of Christ. (1 Cor. 2:10–12, 16)

This is a knowledge of God that, because it is through our union with Christ, is a knowledge of the Father through the Father-Son relationship. It is therefore a saving knowledge, a knowledge of God by grace.

This is a knowledge given to us as faith through the testimony of the Old and New Testaments. First, faith. The Declaration here reflects an ancient theological principle, found especially in St. Augustine, that true knowledge of God is inseparable from love for God and belief in God. John 6:69 recounts the words of Peter, when many friends of Jesus had fled on account of his teaching. Asked why the twelve did not also run away, Peter replies, "we have come to believe and know that you are the Holy One of God." Knowledge of God, because it is participation in Christ's own relationship with the Father, is never independent of the life of faith, of worship, prayer, and the ministry of the Church. There is no "academic" or privileged neutral point of investigation. We will see shortly that this also applies to the proper interpretation of Scripture that is advocated in the Declaration. To grow in knowledge of God we must

---

2. See T. F. Torrance, *The Trinitarian Faith: The Evangelical Theology of the Ancient Catholic Church* (Edinburgh: T. & T. Clark, 1993), p. 53.

stand within the circle of faith, for our faith *is* a sharing in Christ's own knowledge of God. As St. Anselm noted so famously, knowledge of God grows through "faith seeking understanding."[3]

Second, the testimony of Scripture. As the Reformed creedal tradition has been especially firm in asserting, our knowledge of God in Christ is a Scripture-based knowledge. We only know God as Father and Christ as Savior because of the witness of Scripture. The Declaration stands four-square in the tradition that upholds the authority of Scripture. The Reformed tradition consistently rejects private revelations and private interpretations of Scripture. "The apostle Peter has said that the Holy Scriptures are not of private interpretation" declares the *Second Helvetic Confession*, citing 2 Peter 1:20, "and thus we do not allow all possible interpretations" (*BOC*, 5.010). Even powerful personal religious experiences have only secondary significance. All must be brought to Scripture, interpreted by faith, trusting in the Holy Spirit, within the fellowship of the Church. As the Declaration has already insisted, we grow in faith through the preaching of the Word and the celebration of the Word-made-visible in the sacraments.

We turn away from forms of Church life that discount the authority of Scripture or claim knowledge of God that is contrary to the full testimony of Scripture as interpreted by the Holy Spirit working in and through the community of faith across time.

The Declaration follows its affirmation on the authority of Scripture with the statement of intention to reject watered-down approaches to the Bible. The strong words used here make that plain: authority and full testimony leave little room for doubt that the Declaration intends to pull the Church away from theologies that either discount Scripture or claim a knowledge of God contrary to Scripture.

Two problem areas are in view. First, the Declaration stands against the view that Scripture is malleable, yielding its authority to human

---

3. Eugene R. Fairweather, ed. and trans., *A Scholastic Miscellany: Anselm to Ockam* (Philadelphia: The Westminster Press, 1956), p. 70.

experience or to previously adopted points of view. It is not uncommon to hear people of various persuasions argue that when Scripture differs from their convictions, Scripture must be discounted in favor of a more "contemporary" position. That position is roundly rejected in the Declaration. Issues of Christian faith, life, and morals can only have a scriptural basis. There is no other equal authority to lay alongside the Bible.

Second, the Declaration sets out briefly the nature of biblical interpretation that gives a proper framework for debate over Scripture. The problems arise, of course, when all sides claim Scripture as their champion, and we find ourselves debating issues of interpretation. In response to this, the Declaration reemphasizes the classical Reformed position on the *full testimony* of Scripture, as expressed in chapter 1 of *The Westminster Confession of Faith* (*BOC*, 6.009) and chapter 2 of *The Second Helvetic Confession* (*BOC*, 5.010ff.). Paragraph 9 of the first chapter in the *Westminster Confession* sets forth the basic principle: "The infallible rule of interpretation of Scripture, is the Scripture itself" (6.009).

The Declaration also asserts that one ought to read Scripture in the light of Church tradition. This only recognizes the Holy Spirit working in and through the community of faith across time. The *Second Helvetic Confession* affirms that we are not to despise the writings of the theologians of the past, as far as they agree with the Scriptures (*BOC*, 5.011). Similarly, the *Theological Declaration of Barmen* notes that we are to test our words "to see whether they agree with Holy Scripture *and with the Confessions of the Fathers*" (*BOC*, 8.04; italics added). Scripture is to be interpreted today and theological knowledge pursued in serious conversation with the voice of the Church in history. Scripture, and the knowledge of God that arises from Scripture, belongs to the community of faith across time. Through the centuries, the wisdom of interpretation has been guided by the Holy Spirit, consistent with Jesus' promise: "When the Spirit of truth comes, he will guide you into all the truth" (John 16:13). We read Scripture rightly and we do theology properly when we act in accordance with this fact.

Perhaps more controversially, in making the assertion about the community of faith across time, the Declaration also makes a plea to the Church to take back the Scriptures from the academic biblical guilds. Much—though by no means all—technical scholarly biblical study today deliberately operates outside of faith and Church commitments, reading Scripture only as a historic text. The Jesus Seminar is a case in point. The Declaration firmly rejects this approach. The Bible is a theological document par excellence, the product of the Jewish and Christian faiths. The Bible belongs, first of all, to the faith communities who read and interpret it in order to produce transformed lives. Certainly modern biblical scholarship helps to deepen our understanding of the Bible in significant ways, but that scholarly work must be situated within the community of faith that reads prayerfully and thoughtfully, pleads for the guidance of God's Spirit, and, with confidence, claims the Bible as its own. The failure of some biblical scholarship today to read the Bible theologically, in the light of the faith of the Church, is an issue of deep concern.

Sharing in Christ's Love

By our union with Christ we participate in his love of the Father, manifest in his obedience "even unto death on the cross."

"Whoever does not love does not know God, for God is love" (1 John 4:8). The great theological themes of righteousness and the knowledge of God through our union with Christ must finally give way to our sharing in Christ's love of the Father. While believing in Jesus as Lord means a new standing before God and a new knowledge of God, it most assuredly also means a new relationship with God. For if we do not share in Christ's love of the Father, we do not really know the Father.

The great dangers in speaking of the love of God are trivialization and sentimentalization. Love is such an overused and coarsened word today that it carries less and less meaning, even in the Church.

Nevertheless, it is a word we must struggle to reclaim, because it takes us to the heart of the Gospel: love is the nature of Christ's relationship with the Father, and it is this love of the Father and the Son in which we share.

To explicate the meaning and depth of this extraordinary love of God, the Church fathers sometimes used a technical Greek word to describe the mystery of the interior relations within the Holy Trinity: *perichoresis* (*chora*, which means space or room; *chorein*, which means to make room).[4] It refers to the "coindwelling" by which the Persons of the Trinity exist in mutual relationships of love with one another in the unity of the Godhead. The Holy Trinity is the movement of love among the three Persons in the sublime holiness of God's true nature. Staggeringly, this is a love that also goes out to reach us in Christ, and which, through our union with Christ, joins us back to itself, as it were, so that we share in this divine movement of love.

The Declaration states that this love is manifest in Christ's obedience "to the point of death, even death on a cross" (Phil. 2:8). Of course, our Lord had himself laid down the principle that "no one has greater love than this, to lay down one's life for one's friends. You are my friends . . ." (John 15:13–14). Theologically, this is expressed by Paul: "God proves his love for us in that while we still were sinners Christ died for us" (Rom. 5:8). How often Christians get the basic logic of the gospel upside down. God did not send Jesus to die for our sins so that God would love us. Rather, God so loved the world—us—that God sent Jesus to make atonement for our sins. The cross is the action *of* the love of God, not the condition *for* the love of God.

We turn away from any supposed love of God that is manifest apart from a continual longing for and a striving after that loving obedience which Christ offers to God on our behalf.

---

4. See T. F. Torrance, *The Christian Doctrine of God: One Being, Three Persons* (Edinburgh: T. & T. Clark, 1996), p. 102.

Christ's love is a love that went all the way into the hell of our separation from God in order to restore us to union and communion with God. To share in that love by our union with Christ is to share in the fellowship of his suffering. To share in his love of the Father is also to share in his mission from the Father, which is the outpouring of his love for the sake of the world. It is to share in his obedience, for there is no sharing in Christ's love of God without a sharing also in his obedience to the will of God. Love and will are not two things, but the one thing seen from different perspectives. Thus a sharing in Christ's love of the Father means a sharing in what that love led him to do, and to take up our cross daily and follow him. Surely there is no greater desentimentalizing of love than this!

The Declaration intends through and through to be a missional statement. It begins with the mission of God in Jesus Christ. With this statement the Declaration begins a slow shift in focus from God's mission to our mission, or rather, to our sharing in Christ's mission, as the next two sections reflect the transformation of our lives personally, and the transformation of the Church's life in worship and in mission. In Christ, united with Christ, we are awakened from the sloth of self-interest to a life that longs for a deeper conversion in God and a more faithful service of God. We become aware as never before that our hearts are restless until they find their rest in God."[5]

---

5. St. Augustine, *Confessions* (Philadelphia: The Westminster Press, 1960), 1.1.

For Reflection and Discussion

1. Reflect on the theology implied in Heb. 3:1, where we read that Jesus is the "apostle and high priest of our confession." What are the implications, especially of the high priesthood of Jesus, in the development of this section?

2. The Declaration uses the classical Trinitarian naming of God as Father, Son, and Holy Spirit. As explained in the commentary, the word *Father*, when used of God, is to be understood entirely on the basis of the eternal Father-Son relationship in the life of the Trinity. Talk this through in your own words, perhaps with particular reference to John 1:18.

3. What does it mean to participate in Christ's righteousness before God, his knowledge of the Father, and his love of the Father?

4. In what sense does Scripture have authority? How do you see the relationship between the authority of Scripture and an appropriate manner of interpreting or understanding Scripture? Why does the Declaration maintain that Scripture is only properly interpreted within the community of faith?

5. Explore the connection between sharing in Christ's love of the Father and sharing in Christ's fellowship of suffering.

Christ's Life in Us

Overview

Though obscured by our sin, our union with Christ causes his life to shine forth in our lives. This transformation of our lives into the image of Christ is a work of the Holy Spirit begun in this life as a sign and promise of its completion in the life to come.

Section III dealt with some of the effects of our union with Christ—how we come to share in Christ's righteousness before God, as well as in his knowledge and love of the Father. Section IV continues an exploration of these effects, focusing on the doctrine of sanctification (growth in righteousness). As the Holy Spirit unites us with Jesus Christ, his life begins to show itself in our lives. Our actions become more Christlike and our hearts more loving. "It is no longer I who live, but it is Christ who lives in me" (Gal. 2:20).

This process of growth into the image of Christ is not completed in this lifetime. The weight of sin still clings to us, so that our life in Christ this side of glory is a matter of slow progress that is often interrupted, of struggle against our sinful inclinations, of failure and repentance and starting over again. As a preacher once said, "I tried to drown the Old Adam in the waters of baptism, but the miserable wretch can swim!"

In spite of these hindrances, however, our union with Christ *does* bear fruit. The Christian life does involve growth in grace and holiness, even in the face of setbacks and discouragements. This growth, which believers pray and long for, is a gift of the Spirit given in anticipation of that final perfection that we shall enjoy in glory, when our life in Christ is consummated and completed.

Holiness

By our union with Christ our lives participate in the holiness of the One who fulfilled the Law of God on our behalf.

"You shall be holy to me; for I the LORD am holy, and I have separated you from the other peoples to be mine" (Lev. 20:26). To be holy is to be set apart for God, to be caught up in God's purposes, to pray with our Lord, "Thy will be done." Holiness is thus intimately bound up with love of God's Law. As Moses told the Israelites in the territory of Moab: "Because [God] loved your ancestors, he chose their descendants after them. He brought you out of Egypt with his own presence, by his great power. . . . Keep his statutes and his commandments, which I am commanding you today" (Deut. 4:37, 40). "For what other great nation," Moses asks, "has a god so near to it as the LORD our God is whenever we call to him? And what great nation has statutes and ordinances as just as all this entire law that I am setting before you today?" (Deut. 4:7–8). Israel's holiness as a people elected and set apart by God is inseparably connected with her possession of, and love for, God's gift of the Law.

Jesus shows himself to be the Holy One of God precisely by the identification of his own will with the Father's, and this union of wills comes to expression in Jesus' embrace of the deepest purposes of the Law: "Do not think that I have come to abolish the law or the prophets; I have come not to abolish but to fulfill" (Matt. 5:17). Jesus' own holiness shines forth in his matchless love of God and neighbor, a love that perfects and completes the Law.

Our union with Christ involves a sharing in Christ's holiness, and that sharing is inseparable from a conformity of our will to God's will, expressed in (but not limited to!) a love of God's Law. We embrace the Law not as the means of our salvation, which has been freely given to us in Christ, but as the proper expression of our thankfulness and the outward manifestation of our union with Christ in the power of the Holy Spirit. "All who obey his commandments abide in him, and he abides in them. And by this we know that he abides in us, by the Spirit that he has given us" (1 John 3:24).

We turn away from forms of Church life that ignore Christ's call to a life of holiness, or that seek to pit Law and Gospel against one another as if both were not expressions of the one Word of God.

Recognizing holiness as the authentic fruit of a life united with Christ, the Declaration here turns us away from counterfeit versions of Christian faith that embrace the forgiveness that Christ holds out to sinners while ignoring or rejecting the healing from sinfulness that he also brings. Dietrich Bonhoeffer, a German theologian martyred under the Nazis, had a name for this distortion of Christianity. Bonhoeffer called it "cheap grace." He wrote:

> Instead of following Christ, let the Christian enjoy the consolations of his grace! That is what we mean by cheap grace, the grace which amounts to the justification of the sin without the justification of the repentant sinner who departs from sin and from whom sin departs. Cheap grace is not the kind of forgiveness of sin which frees us from the toils of sin. Cheap grace is the grace we bestow on ourselves.
>
> Cheap grace is the preaching of forgiveness without requiring repentance, baptism without church discipline, Communion without confession, absolution without personal

confession. Cheap grace is grace without discipleship, grace without the cross, grace without Jesus Christ, living and incarnate."[1]

To profess Christian faith and yet continue to bask comfortably in an unexamined and unamended life is to follow a false Christ who has no power to heal or save.

One of the ways this false Christ insinuates his way into the Church in our time is through a distorted understanding of the relationship between Law and Gospel. This false understanding sees the Gospel as *opposed* to the Law, as doing away with the Law and its requirements so that under the Gospel one may now go on living as one always has, but with the comforting assurance that one is now forgiven by God and accepted "just the way I am"—in all one's pride, rebellion, and self-absorption!

Like most heresies, this one has a grain of truth at its center. The Gospel *does* do away with the Law in a certain sense: Because of the grace extended to us in Christ, the power of the Law to condemn us has been taken away and overcome. It is also the case that with the coming of Christ, we look now to him as the ground of our salvation rather than to our own adherence to the Law. This is what Paul was insisting on so strongly in his letter to the Galatians. But the *result* of these gifts of grace is not to nullify the Law, as though God were now so satisfied and pleased with our sinfulness as to pronounce a divine "Never mind!" regarding his commandments. Rather, the grace offered us in Christ restores the Law to its proper function in the life of believers, making it no longer an enemy that condemns us, nor a means by which we try to save ourselves apart from God, but an expression of our thankfulness. Christ's coming frees us to use the Law—and love the Law!—as a means of glorifying God and expressing our gratitude to him. In the words of the *Westminster Confession*,

---

1. Dietrich Bonhoeffer, *The Cost of Discipleship* (New York: The MacMillan Company, 1961), p. 36.

Good works, done in obedience to God's commandments, are the fruits and evidences of a true and lively faith: and by them believers manifest their thankfulness, strengthen their assurance, edify their brethren, adorn the profession of the gospel, stop the mouths of the adversaries, and glorify God, whose workmanship they are, created in Christ Jesus thereunto, that, having their fruit unto holiness, they may have the end, eternal life. (*BOC*, 6.088)

The Law paints for us a picture of that perfect love of God and neighbor that is the goal of our life in Christ. The Declaration roundly rejects any forms of Church life that would ignore that goal or turn us away from it.

Sexual Purity

By our union with Christ we participate in his obedience. In these times of moral and sexual confusion we affirm the consistent teaching of Scripture that calls us to chastity outside of marriage and faithfulness within the covenant of marriage between a man and a woman.

This paragraph may strike the reader as an interruption in the flow of the text of the Declaration, but actually it relates to the teaching on holiness in the preceding paragraphs. This paragraph and the next apply the teaching of the Declaration to a particular issue confronting the Church at this point in its history. This "interruption" in the flow of the Declaration mirrors the disruption in the flow of Church life brought about by disputes and disagreements over sexual morality. As such it reflects the very particular historical circumstances—a renewal movement initially formed and galvanized around efforts to secure the Church's historic teachings on sexual morality—that led to the writing of the Declaration.

It is important to keep in mind at this point the difference between a declaration and a confession as explained in the introduction. The Declaration is not intended to be a complete summary of the whole of Christian doctrine; nor does it seek to set forth a comprehensive response to all the challenges facing the Church in our day. That this one issue receives attention at this point in the text reflects the specific historical circumstances of the Declaration's formulation; it is *not* intended to suggest that this particular issue stands preeminent among all the challenges facing the Church at this point in history. For all the scandal and notoriety that regularly attach to sexual sins, far more damage has been done historically to the communities and institutions of civilized society by the operations of simple human greed! The reference in the text to *"moral and* sexual confusion" refers to the wide scope of challenges facing the Christian community today.

This paragraph also reflects the Declaration's particular approach to the Bible set forth in section III. The reference to the "consistent teaching of Scripture" *could* be a problem were the interpretation of Scripture undertaken in a vacuum. Competing claims about the proper interpretation of particular Scripture passages touching on questions of homosexual practice among Christians have figured very prominently in the debates about sexual morality that have vexed the Church in recent years. The Declaration takes its stand on "the full testimony of Scripture as interpreted by the Holy Spirit working in and through the community of faith across time." On this view one may argue that throughout history (and among the vast majority of Christian communions in existence today) the disputed Scripture passages have been consistently interpreted by the Church as condemning homosexual practice among Christian believers. By taking its stand on consistent historical understandings of the Bible within the Christian community, the Declaration is here able to offer a clear and forthright statement in the midst of the tangled web of competing "readings" of the Bible that characterize our modern era.

We turn away from forms of Church life that fail to pray for and strive after a rightly ordered sexuality as the gracious gift of a loving God, offered to us in Christ by the power of the Holy Spirit. We also turn away from forms of Church life that fail to forgive and restore those who repent of sexual and other sins.

The Declaration here presents the negative counterpart of its positive statement about Christian sexual morality. It is important to note carefully the image of the Christian life that is being set forth. Echoing the language in section II, which associates authentic discipleship with the determination to "pray, hope and strive for a life that is pleasing to God," the Declaration here paints a picture of the Christian life in terms of longing for and growth toward perfection rather than its full attainment in this life.

Indeed, when we consider Jesus' warning that a lustful look at a member of the opposite sex is tantamount to adultery (Matt. 5:27–28), and reflect on New Testament descriptions of the marriage bond as an image of that perfect love that binds Christ and his Church (Eph. 5:31–33), it is clear that few if any among us can claim to fully possess a "rightly ordered sexuality" of the sort the Scriptures have in mind. But in Christ this gift is genuinely offered and promised to us. The eminent Swiss theologian Karl Barth observed that every "You shall!" of the Law contains within itself the promise, "You shall *be!*"[2] So it is here. We recognize (joyfully) in these daunting New Testament teachings the image and promise of what our troubled and troubling sexual natures *will be* when finally we are perfected in glory.

In the meantime, we all repent, strive, pray, and hope in reliance on the grace and promise of God: "Blessed are those who hunger and thirst for righteousness, for they will be filled" (Matt. 5:6). It is this hungering and thirsting for righteousness, rather than any specific degree of its attainment, that the Declaration sets forth as an essential mark of life in Christ.

Finally, it is worth pondering the scope of this striving, praying, and hoping in our contemporary social context. The language of chastity and faithfulness that appears in this section of the Declaration has figured prominently in debates about the ordination of homosexuals in recent times. But the Bible's descriptions of a "rightly ordered sexuality" have at

2. Karl Barth, *Community, State, and Church: Three Essays* (Garden City, NY: Anchor Books, 1960), p. 78.

least as much critical light to cast on the divorce epidemic and the problems of broken families in our society and church as they do on issues of sexual orientation. Surely one of the concrete manifestations of the church's hungering and thirsting for righteousness in this area needs to be a sustained and focused attention to the task of nurturing and supporting strong and faithful marriages and families.

For Reflection and Discussion

1. What does it mean that Jesus is the Holy One of God (John 6:69)? What are the implications for our holiness? (Remember to work this through in the light of our union in Christ.)

2. Explain in your own words the relationship between Law and Gospel.

3. Why does the Declaration insert a statement on "moral and sexual confusion"? How do you respond to the reaffirmation of the traditional teaching of the Church—and the teaching of the PC(USA)—in regard to marriage between a man and a woman?

4. What role does prayer have in your congregation for those who struggle with sexual issues and practices? What would be the practical results of forgiveness and "restoration"?

5. What does your church do to strengthen marriage and family life and to support and assist single persons in faithful and upright living? What could or should the church be doing in these areas?

Section V

The Church as the Body of Christ

Overview

As the Body of Christ the Church has her life in Christ.

Up to this point the Declaration has been spelling out the consequences for individual believers of our union with Christ. In this section the focus shifts toward the consequences of that union for the Church as a whole. Paul's teaching that the Church is the Body of Christ means that our life together in the Church is lived "in Christ," and therefore is decisively shaped by our union with one another in him (Rom. 12:4–5; 1 Cor. 12:27).

The Unity of the Church

By our union with Christ the Church binds together believers in every time and place.

"We are one in the Spirit, we are one in the Lord." The words of the familiar hymn "They'll Know We Are Christians by Our Love" express the ancient Christian confession of the oneness of the true Church, the Body of Christ, in every time and place. As the *Second Helvetic Confession* puts it,

> Since there is always but one God, and there is one mediator between God and men, Jesus the Messiah, and one Shepherd of the whole flock, one Head of this body, and, to conclude, one Spirit, one salvation, one faith, one Testament or covenant, it necessarily follows that there is only one Church. (*BOC*, 5.126)

We confess unity with *believers* in every time and place. This unity is grounded in the fact that we are all joined to Christ in faith by the power of the Spirit.

This confession contrasts markedly with the popular piety of twentieth-century American Protestantism. People at the turn of the last century were very optimistic about worldwide progress toward a peaceful and unified humanity, held together by the rational recognition of our common membership in the human family. Indeed, some progress has been made toward achieving these humanitarian ideals. Nevertheless, looking back on the twentieth century, the bloodiest century in recorded history, we see that the dream of a world united around common humanitarian ideals seems farther away now than it did in the year 1900. The history of the twentieth century is replete with cultural fragmentation and conflict. Around the world, ancient ethnic, tribal, and national divisions have reasserted themselves with a ferocity that brushes aside philosophical appeals to our common humanity.

Jesus Christ *is* the only power strong enough to unite all the members of the human race across the many walls that divide us! Jesus Christ is the hope of the world. The Church has a powerful witness to make here, both to our own society and to the world at large, as the Spirit helps us live into the oneness that is ours in Christ. Our union with him and in him transcends and overrules every lesser loyalty that threatens to separate us from other brothers and sisters in Christ. We should be praying daily that God will give to all the churches the grace to live out this truth of our confession!

We turn away from forms of Church life that identify the true Church only with particular styles of worship, polity, or institutional structure. We also turn away from forms of Church life that ignore the witness of those who have gone before us.

With the confession of our unity with one another in Christ, the Declaration here turns us away from attitudes and practices within the Church that fasten so tenaciously on differences in the outward forms of Church life as to lose sight of the transcendent unity that binds all of us together. We hear from various quarters these days that churches who use contemporary music in their services are "not really Reformed." From other directions come accusations that churches using more traditional liturgies "have abandoned the missionary task." Over against every sort of parochialism and provincialism that identifies one's own way of doing things as the exclusive way of the one true Church, we here affirm our essential unity in Christ with all who believe him and confess him Lord.

This is not to say that Christians may not legitimately enter into debates about the most appropriate forms of worship and Church life in any given cultural setting. But we here reject the notion that such debates are anything other than family discussions among brothers and sisters in Christ. Our union in Christ transcends the outward differences that characterize the life of our various churches.

One often overlooked way by which we in the Church sometimes deny our unity with other believers is our refusal to take seriously the witness of Christians who have gone before us, as if nothing worth listening to could ever come from people of the past. The possession of color televisions and microwave ovens is no guarantee of wisdom in matters of the spirit! This bigoted attitude that automatically rejects the wisdom of the past is reflected in the widespread ignorance and neglect of our theological tradition that so sadly characterizes our churches in these times.

The Declaration here encourages a reverence for, and serious dialogue with, those who have gone before us in the faith. They, too, are our brothers and sisters in Christ, no less than faithful Christians of other denominations. Here we find echoes of the theme that we noted in the discussion of scriptural interpretation in section III: We attend to the guidance of the Holy Spirit who works in and through the community of faith *across time*. In Christ we are united with faithful believers in every age and time—and beyond time! That means the voices of our theological heritage should be primary conversation partners as we reflect on the shape and form of faithfulness in our own age and time.

The Catholicity of the Church

By our union with Christ the Church is called out into particular communities of worship and mission.

A character in the *Peanuts* comic strip once declared, "I love mankind—it's people I can't stand!"[1] For Christians it is often easier to love the neighbor who is halfway around the world than the one who is sitting in the next pew. But the Declaration here affirms that the oneness in Christ we have been confessing is no airy or abstract thing, existing only in the realm of vague sentiments and spiritual ideals. Like the Word himself, our unity in Christ takes on flesh and blood, confronting us in the form of a real and tangible connection with this particular sister or brother in the life of this particular church. This makes it harder to be a follower of Jesus sometimes. It is often easier to love persons in the abstract, safely removed from their temperamental quirks and peculiar ideas that sometimes get on our nerves. But just as our union in Christ stands over all the political and ethnic and economic differences that threaten to divide us, so our union in Christ also overcomes the personal and temperamental divisions that stand as potential barriers between us and our neighbors. That union is given concrete form by our life together with the sisters and brothers of our own

---

1. Robert L. Short, *The Gospel According to Peanuts* (Richmond: John Knox Press, 1965), p. 122.

worshiping and serving congregations. "We know that we have passed from death to life because we love one another. Whoever does not love abides in death" (1 John 3:14).

In affirming that our union with Christ is responsible for calling the church into particular communities of worship and mission, the Declaration is also making the claim that individual congregations are more than just voluntary associations of like-minded individuals. Rather, the church is a divine as well as a human institution, and it is in fact the power of the risen Christ in our midst that gives rise to these particular communities of faith, mission, and worship.

We turn away from forms of Church life that see the work of the local congregation as sufficient unto itself, as if it were not a local representation of the one, holy, catholic, and apostolic Church called together by the power of the Spirit in every age and time until our Lord returns.

The Declaration here turns us away from the false conclusion, drawn from the Church's existence in particular local communities, that such local congregations are independent organizations that are essentially separate from one another. The Declaration here affirms the ancient confession, reflected in the Nicene Creed, that the Church is catholic, or universal. Each congregation represents, in however splendid or modest a way, the local presence of the universal Church.

This is a heartening affirmation for smaller congregations, which sometimes have a tendency to feel illegitimate—like less of a church— because they cannot boast the impressive budgets, facilities, programs, and attendance of larger churches. Over against every such attempt to rank individual churches as greater or lesser, the Declaration here affirms that even the most modest of congregations embodies in its own place and in its own manner the full reality and presence of the one, holy, catholic, and apostolic Church, the body of Christ. "For where two or three are gathered in my name, I am there among them" (Matt. 18:20).

This is also an important affirmation of the Presbyterian connectional system. Our Church polity is founded on this understanding that local congregations are not isolated, independent units. We are all connected to one another by our union in Christ; we all need one another in order to be the true Body of Jesus Christ in the world. Any sort of sectarian or factional spirit that seeks to "go its own way" in separation from the rest of the Church is here repudiated. There is no such thing as an "independent" Presbyterian Church!

There is also a critical edge to this renunciation. It perhaps should lead us to call into question the denominational stewardship practices that have left multitudes of smaller, rural congregations struggling for survival and bereft of pastoral leadership, while larger, stronger churches and governing bodies continue to allocate resources as though oblivious to this plight of their brothers and sisters.

Also, if we affirm the essential oneness of every Presbyterian congregation by its connection to the one Body of Christ, no biblical or logical grounds exist by which we can draw the limits of our unity at the boundaries of Presbyterianism. Our union in Christ unites us not only with other Presbyterians but with faithful Christians of every denomination. This commits us irrevocably to the ecumenical quest, if not to any particular institutional means for pursuing it. Jesus' high-priestly prayer captures well what we should all be praying, hoping, and striving toward: "that they may all be one. As you, Father, are in me and I am in you, may they also be in us, so that the world may believe that you have sent me" (John 17:21).

The Mission of the Church

By our union with Christ our lives participate in God's mission to the world. . . .

The Declaration here moves toward its conclusion with a ringing affirmation of the *missional character of the Church*. If Christ is God's gracious mission to the world, as set forth in section I, and if the Church is united with him, then it follows necessarily that the Church shares in every aspect of Christ's mission. The descriptions of the Church's mission that follow in this paragraph are intended to be suggestive rather than exhaustive, but it is still worth attending to the particulars there set forth. The artificial distinction between evangelism and humanitarian mission is rejected. In Christ, God has come to redeem every aspect of human existence. To claim that the Church's mission embodied only the spiritual aspect of God's compassion, or only the social or economic aspects, would be to deny the Church's union with Christ. The Declaration then lists some representative aspects of that encompassing mission of God in Christ.

1. *To uphold the value of every human life.* Every human being the Church encounters, whether within or without its own walls, is a person for whom Christ died. God's gracious "yes" to humankind, uttered in Jesus Christ, is intended for every single human being: rich and poor, powerless and powerful, born and unborn, old and young, healthy and sick, criminal and law-abiding, able and disabled. There are no limits to the compassion God has shown toward the human race in Jesus Christ, and so there can be no limits on the scope of the Church's mission in union with Christ to the whole of the human family. This is not to say, of course, that any particular congregation or Christian individual is obligated to reach out in all these ways. God distributes different gifts and vocations to different parts of the Body, for the good of the whole (1 Cor. 12ff.). This underscores what little sense it would make to think of any single congregation as an isolated and independent unit! Individuals and congregations have their own special vocations within the Body of Christ, but considered as a whole there is no limiting or confining the scope of the Church's mission to the human race, just as there is no limit to the love God has shown to us in Jesus Christ.

2. *To make disciples of all peoples.* The love and forgiveness and new life that God extends to the human race in Jesus Christ is intended for everyone. "As I live, says the Lord GOD, I have no pleasure in the death of the wicked, but that the wicked turn from their ways and live" (Ezek. 33:11). And if Jesus Christ *is* in his own person this love and forgiveness and new life, this missional turn of God outward toward his fallen creation,

then nothing could be more inhuman and unloving than to withhold the proclamation of Christ from any of the world's peoples. By its confession of Jesus Christ in section I, the Declaration has ruled out any sort of view that posits the existence of "many paths to God" apart from Jesus Christ. Here we see the consequences of that confession spelled out in a commitment to universal evangelism.

3. *To establish Christ's justice and peace in all creation.* In Jesus' resurrection from the dead, we witness the first fruits of the *new creation* that God has inaugurated in him.

> They shall not labor in vain,
> or bear children for calamity;
> for they shall be the offspring
> blessed by the LORD—
> and their descendants as well.
> Before they call I will answer,
> while they are yet speaking I will hear.
> The wolf and the lamb shall feed together,
> the lion shall eat straw like the ox;
> but the serpent—its food shall be dust!
> They shall not hurt or destroy
> on all my holy mountain,
> says the LORD. (Isa. 65:23–25)

The kingdom of God that dawns among us in Jesus Christ is a kingdom of *Shalom*—of benevolent order and peace and goodness in every sphere of relation among human beings, God, and the created world. Shalom is the order of the world as God intended it from the beginning.

Christ comes to us as the bearer of this Shalom and the firstfruits of God's promised restoration of all things. And so the Church that lives in union with him prays and hopes and works toward this Shalom in every aspect of its earthly existence. This affirmation resonates deeply with our Reformed heritage, which lists "the promotion of social righteousness" and "the exhibition of the Kingdom of Heaven to the world" among the Great Ends of the Church.

4. *To secure that visible oneness in Christ that is the promised inheritance of every believer.* Here the Declaration makes explicit the ecumenical commitment that we discussed in connection with the preceding paragraph. The division of the Christian churches stands as a scandalous contradiction of that very union in Christ that we have been confessing all through the Declaration. A church that takes such a confession seriously cannot but commit to the long, hard work of prayer and dialogue and forgiveness and reconciliation required to address the divisions that presently distort and disfigure the Body of Christ in the world. This means some serious soul-searching for us Protestants, especially, who have all too often tended to respond to disagreements within the life of the Church by starting new denominations. Perhaps a significant part of this ecumenical commitment for us entails a refusal to become any more divided than we already are!

In closing our discussion of this paragraph, the organic relation that exists between the various aspects of mission described here is worth noting. We place the highest possible value on the life of our fellow human beings by inviting them to join us in the fellowship of Christ's disciples; and as our evangelistic efforts move closer toward the goal of an entire world bound together in Christ within the fellowship of a reunited Church, we catch a glimpse of the kind of Shalom that God promises among human beings when the Kingdom of Heaven will be established in its fullness. All of these dimensions of mission are really interrelated aspects of the one mission of reconciliation and redemption that God has undertaken in Jesus Christ!

We turn away from forms of Church life that fail to bear witness in word and deed to Christ's compassion and peace, and the Gospel of salvation.

The Declaration here turns us away from nonmissional understandings of the Church. God's mission to the world, the person of Jesus Christ, and the calling of the Church are inseparable. None of these terms can be understood apart from the others. We understand God's mission to the world only as we understand what God has done in Jesus Christ and continues to do in and through the Church's work in the power of the Holy Spirit. We understand who Jesus is only as we come to see him as God's gracious mission to and for the world, continuing even now in the mission of the Church, which is his Body. Likewise, we understand what the Church is only as we see its union with Christ in the power of the Spirit and its consequent participation in God's mission to the world in Christ.

The Declaration rejects any and all forms of Church life that turn congregations inward on themselves, generating a preoccupation with the perpetuation of their own existence and the delivery of services to their own members only. Rather, the Declaration insists, the Church *is* the church only as it embodies God's mission to the world in Christ.

The Declaration also turns us away from understandings of the Church's calling that fail to reflect the fullness of God's redemptive purposes in Christ. To focus exclusively on "social action" ministries to the exclusion of evangelistic witness is to fall short of God's mission to the world in Christ. The same is true of ministries that focus exclusively on "spiritual matters" without ever addressing how the structures and practices of society may become better vehicles for the justice, compassion, and peace that God wills for every human being. As we said earlier, this does not mean that every particular congregation and agency of the Church has to embody each of these emphases in equal proportions in its ministry—there are varieties of gifts and callings within the one Body of Christ. But it does warn us away from understandings of the *whole* Church's calling that fail to reflect the fullness of God's graciousness toward the world in Jesus Christ.

The Hope of the Church

By our union with Christ the Church participates in Christ's resurrected life and awaits in hope the future that God has prepared for her. Even so come quickly, Lord Jesus!

The Declaration ends on a note of hope and promise. The confession we have made here is not a program of action we have resolved to undertake on the basis of our own strength. It is not some new programmatic emphasis to guide our busyness from day to day. It is a confession, rather, of the way things *are*: the true nature of the Church in union with our Lord and Savior Jesus Christ. Martin Luther was absolutely right when he wrote, in the words of the familiar hymn, "Did we in our own strength confide, our striving would be losing." But the future that awaits us is not the end product of our own (often misguided) labors, thank heaven, but the redemption of all things in Christ. Our life in the present is not an exercise in laborious righteousness, weighted down by the oppressive consciousness that everything rests on our shoulders. Rather, our present pilgrimage is a joyous embrace of the promise that God is at work to make all things new in Christ, and the astonished and thankful recognition that God has gifted us with a participation in that work of redemption by our union with his Son in the power of the Holy Spirit. Paul's doxology here seems utterly appropriate (Rom. 11:33, 36): "O the depth of the riches and wisdom and knowledge of God! How unsearchable are his judgments and how inscrutable his ways! . . . For from him and through him and to him are all things. To him be glory forever. Amen."

In the name of the Father, and of the Son, and of the Holy Spirit.

The affirmations and renunciations of the Declaration are here offered in the Trinitarian Name, marking it as a document anchored firmly in the Bible, as interpreted by the Holy Spirit in the great tradition of the apostolic Church. This final statement also locates the Declaration's act of confession within the joyous history of the Triune God's gracious encounter with our poor, lost world. As the grace and mercy of God reach out to us *from* the Father, *through* the Son, *in* the power of the Holy Spirit, so our joyous response to the divine goodness rises to the Father, with the Son, by the acting of that same Spirit.

By our union with Christ, the Declaration thus joins itself—not on account of its own highly questionable merits, but as a pure gift of God's grace—with the perfect praise that the Son eternally renders to the Father on our behalf. It thus assumes its place, however modest, in the unending chorus of praise that rises to the throne of God from the lips of the faithful, on behalf of all creation. Together we pray that God may be pleased with our humble Declaration, offered in the Spirit as an act of praise and thanksgiving, and ask in the name of Jesus Christ that God make use of it in ways that bring glory to his Name.